J. C. BUSH SCHOOL

Lewis and Clark:

Explorers of the
Louisiana Purchase

J. C. BUSH SCHOOL

Explorers of New Worlds

Lewis and Clark:

Explorers of the Louisiana Purchase

Richard Kozar

Chelsea House Publishers
Philadelphia

Prepared for Chelsea House Publishers by:
OTTN Publishing, Warminster, PA

CHELSEA HOUSE PUBLISHERS
Editor in Chief: Stephen Reginald
Managing Editor: James D. Gallagher
Production Manager: Pamela Loos
Art Director: Sara Davis
Director of Photography: Judy L. Hasday
Senior Production Editor: LeeAnne Gelletly
Series Designer: Keith Trego

http://www.chelseahouse.com

3 5 7 9 8 6 4 2

Library of Congress Cataloging-in-Publication Data

Kozar, Richard.
    Lewis and Clark / by Richard F. Kozar.
p.   cm. – (Explorers of new worlds)
Includes bibliographical references and index.
Summary: A biography of the team who explored the
Louisiana Purchase territory while seeking the elusive
Northwest Passage to the Pacific Ocean.
ISBN 0-7910-5513-2 (hc)
1. Lewis, Meriwether, 1774–1809 Juvenile literature.
Clark, William, 1770–1838 Juvenile literature. 3. Explor-
ers–West (U.S.)–Biography Juvenile literature. 4. Lewis
and Clark Expedition (1804–06) Juvenile literature. 5.
West (U.S.)–Discovery and exploration Juvenile litera-
ture. 6. West (U.S.)–Description and travel Juvenile liter-
ature. [1. Lewis, Meriwether, 1774–1809. 2. Clark,
William, 1770–1838. 3. Explorers. 4. Lewis and Clark
Expedition (1804–1806). 5. West (U.S.)–Discovery and
exploration.] I. Title. II. Series.
F592.7.L42K69   1999
917.804'2–dc21   99-35227
                                                          CIP

Publisher's Note: Some quotations in this book come
from original documents and letters written by Lewis
and Clark. These quotations include the writing incon-
sistencies and spelling errors of the original documents.

Contents

William Clark was one of the two men chosen to lead the Corps of Discovery into the unknown wilderness of the American Northwest. Clark and his partner, Meriwether Lewis, bravely led a small band across the continent to reach the Pacific Ocean.

Into the Unknown I

When we think of famous explorers, people like Christopher Columbus, Ferdinand Magellan, and Marco Polo come to mind. All were Europeans, and all struck out hoping to find trade routes and riches. Columbus, for example, was sent by the queen of Spain to find a westward trade route across the Atlantic Ocean to the Far East. But, like several other world travelers, he ended up finding something totally unexpected—in his case, the "New World," which Europeans didn't even know existed.

Centuries after Columbus first crossed the Atlantic Ocean, America would have explorers of its own. Like the earlier Europeans, these people boldly traveled into the unknown. They would discover not what lay across wide oceans, but what lay up mighty rivers, across vast plains, and beyond towering mountain ranges. They would explore the vast and wondrous lands between the east and west coasts of America.

Among all of America's explorers, perhaps none are more famous than Meriwether Lewis and William Clark, who are often referred to in history books as simply "Lewis and Clark." Unlike Columbus, these two former soldiers didn't sail the high seas on their historic adventure, which began in 1804. But their journey did involve navigating treacherous, uncharted rivers inside the continental United States. What they found during their epic journey of exploration included majestic landscapes, wild animals never before seen by white men, and a variety of Native American tribes.

Meriwether Lewis, William Clark, and several dozen other men who joined the adventure came to be known as the Corps of Discovery. A *corps* (pronounced "cor") is a group of people, often soldiers, who act together for a common goal. Lewis and Clark were former soldiers, but several of the men in their party had no military background at all. The men in the Corps of Discovery came from all walks of life and from many American states. One especially valuable person who joined the **expedition** was an Native American woman. Her name was Sacagawea, and she carried her infant child nearly the entire length of the Corps of Discovery's 28-month, 8,000-plus-mile trip.

Like Columbus's voyage, Lewis and Clark's original quest turned out to be something of a failure. They were searching for the fabled Northwest Passage, a long-sought trade route. The Northwest Passage would allow valuable goods such as animal furs to be transported from the unsettled northwestern half of America by river to St. Louis. At the time, St. Louis (in present-day Missouri) was the farthest edge of civilization. What Lewis and Clark discovered was that there was no easy water route to reach the Pacific coast of America via the Missouri River. Blocking the way were the mighty Rocky Mountains. Although the existence of the Rockies had been known, the mountains were far taller and wider than anyone but the Indians could imagine.

But Lewis and Clark's journey wasn't really a failure. Even their not finding the Northwest Passage had some benefits. It led explorers to search for other routes across the continent. And Lewis and Clark proved that the trip to the Pacific was possible, even if it was difficult and often dangerous.

The diaries the two leaders kept of their journey revealed a great deal about Native Americans as well as the amazing diversity of plants, animals, and countryside the explorers saw along the way. And the Corps of Discovery mapped their route so well that it served as a guide to opening up the western frontier to further exploration and settlement.

Of course, many historians have pointed out that by opening a gateway to the frontier, Lewis and Clark paved the way for America's conquest of Great Plains and Western Indian tribes. The Indians would be outmanned and outgunned by the U.S. Army and pioneers hungry to harvest furs, mine gold, and plant crops in western regions. And thanks to careless overhunting by whites who came after Lewis and Clark, the American buffalo was nearly extinct by the late 1800s.

But pushing back Indian nations and killing off the buffalo certainly were not the intentions of Lewis and Clark, or of President Thomas Jefferson, who *commissioned* the expedition. Jefferson, who considered the expedition a quest for knowledge,

Thomas Jefferson, the third president of the United States, was always interested in learning. He saw the mission of Lewis and Clark as a quest for knowledge.

had dreamed of it for 20 years. Of course, he hoped that Lewis and Clark's **trek** would boost America's economy by allowing settlers to head west and transport trade goods back to the heartland of America.

And he also directed Lewis and Clark to declare to all they met that the United States was now the owner of the Louisiana Territory, a huge tract of land it had purchased in 1804 from Napoleon, the emperor of France. The Louisiana Purchase added a great deal of land to the United States: from the Gulf Coast as far west as the border of what is now

The first page of the Louisiana Purchase. The 1804 agreement with France allowed the United States to double its size by buying a vast territory for $15 million.

Idaho and Montana, and as far north as the upper part of Montana. (At this point in U.S. history, midwestern and western states had not yet been established and named, and Texas, New Mexico, and California were still owned by the Spanish.)

But Jefferson was equally interested in learning more about the Indians. He wanted to know their language, homes, customs, and views of the white man, because he hoped the United States could become trading partners with them. He even went so far as to extend an open invitation to the Indian chiefs to come to Washington, D.C., and visit him at the U.S. government's expense.

Jefferson was also greatly interested in the geography and natural resources of the uncharted West. He directed expedition members to keep careful records of the birds, plants, fish, and animals they discovered along the way.

Thanks to Lewis and Clark, Jefferson and other American citizens got their first glimpse of the prairie dog (Clark called it a "barking squirrel") that lived by the thousands in the prairies and northern deserts of the West. The gopherlike critter was captured and sent alive back east by Lewis and Clark's group. The men had hauled buckets and buckets of

Missouri River water to flush one of the animals out from the amazing network of dens and tunnels prairie dogs dig. Also shipped to the president were live magpies (crowlike birds) along with the hides, antlers, and bones of never-before-seen creatures such as pronghorn antelope and the awesome grizzly bear.

Were it not for these animal specimens sent back by the expedition, American citizens may have simply dismissed the descriptions of such wondrous creatures as "tall tales." After all, what early peoples didn't know, they were prone to make up. For example, North American settlers from various countries were fond of believing that a western tribe of Native Americans had descended from an early Welsh prince named Madoc. (Welshmen come from Wales, a region in Great Britain.) Stories had been passed down for gen-

In 1783, Thomas Jefferson had asked a famous frontiersman named George Rogers Clark to explore the land west of the Mississippi River. Clark, a Revolutionary War hero, turned him down. Ten years later, Jefferson sponsored the exploration of Frenchman André Michaux, but that mission failed.

erations of a fair-skinned, blue-eyed Indian tribe known as the Madocians. However, Lewis and Clark found no such people, although they did learn that the Indian nations were made up of completely separate tribes with different appearances and customs.

Thus, Lewis and Clark made a great contribution to American history, not because of what they set out to find (an easy Northwest Passage to the Pacific) or what they thought they would find (Welsh Indians). Rather, their importance lies in what they saw and described and mapped: a huge, wild land where no white man had gone before.

Twenty-nine-year-old Meriwether Lewis was Thomas Jefferson's choice as commander of the Corps of Discovery in 1803. Lewis had served as Jefferson's private secretary before being selected to lead the exploring party westward.

The Mission and Its Men 2

homas Jefferson would have earned a important place in American history even if he had never become president. In 1776, he wrote the Declaration of Independence, which laid out for American patriots—and the world—the reasons America was fighting for independence from Great Britain in the Revolutionary War.

Jefferson was, quite simply, a master at writing words. And he took great pains to pen elaborate instructions for Meriwether Lewis before the explorer set off on his journey up the Missouri River. "The object of your mission," the president wrote on June 20, 1803, "is to explore the

Missouri River, and such principal stream[s] of it, as by its course and communication with the waters of the Pacific ocean . . . may offer the most direct & practicable water communication across the continent."

It wasn't the first time America's third president had encouraged someone to look for the Northwest Passage. Two decades earlier, he had tried to convince William Clark's older brother, Revolutionary War hero George Rogers Clark, to head up the Missouri—with no luck. But when Jefferson became president in 1801, he had even more reason to sponsor such an expedition: a Canadian fur trapper named Alexander Mackenzie had completed a similar trek through western Canada to the Pacific in 1793, giving the British colony a strong claim to parts of the Northwest as well as to its bountiful fur trade.

When the United States completed the Louisiana Purchase on March 10, 1804, the nation's size doubled. And Jefferson felt compelled to send scouts into the Western frontier to announce America's rightful claim to the inhabitants there. The scouting party would also take the opportunity to map travel routes through the wilderness, make note of the terrain and whether it was suited for farming, and meet

Alexander Mackenzie, a young fur trapper, traveled through Canada to the Pacific Ocean, carving this inscription on a rock there. He later published the story of his journey. Mackenzie's book inspired President Jefferson to send his own expedition into the Northwest.

with Indian tribes to learn which were friendly and which were hostile.

Jefferson's first choice for the mission this time around was Meriwether Lewis, who was a relatively young 29 in 1803. Lewis had grown up in Virginia, not far from Jefferson's own home at Monticello. Because of their common love of natural history, the two had become acquaintances. Lewis joined the U.S. militia (a citizens' army) in 1794 and eventually became a captain in the regular army in 1800. Although he never fought in any wars, he did have opportunities to meet and deal with various Native American tribes while performing his duties. And it was while Lewis was serving in the army that he met William Clark, who was his superior officer for a short time. The two quickly became close friends.

Benjamin Rush, a well-known doctor who practiced in Philadelphia, provided advice and medical training for the members of the Corps of Discovery.

After Jefferson became president in 1801, he asked Lewis to become his personal **secretary**. Jefferson was almost certainly grooming Lewis for the search for the Northwest Passage. The well-educated president encouraged Lewis, who had no formal education, to help himself to the many books in Jefferson's personal library at Monticello. At the time, Jefferson's collection of books was the largest private collection in America. He clearly wanted his young student to become versed in subjects like **botany**, medicine, **astronomy**, and mapmaking.

Jefferson also sent Lewis to meet with some of the brightest minds in the young country. In Lancaster, Pennsylvania, Lewis met astronomer Andrew Ellicott, who taught the young Virginian how to use the stars to measure his position in the uncharted wilderness.

Next, Lewis traveled to Philadelphia for some medical tutoring by renowned doctor Benjamin Rush. Rush gave the Corps of Discovery leader lessons in "bleeding"–cutting patients and allowing them to bleed. At the time, this procedure was thought to relieve a variety of ailments. Another questionable remedy that Rush recommended for all that might ail a person was homemade **laxatives** nicknamed "Rush's thunderbolts."

Lewis then met with Philadelphia professor Caspar Wistar, who was an expert in fossils and human anatomy (the body's parts).

All of these learned men were personal friends of Jefferson. They helped to prepare Lewis for the assorted challenges he would face leading several dozen men through the wilderness. The very lives of the expedition's members might depend on the skills and knowledge their leader picked up in a few short weeks.

But Lewis also needed to obtain equipment as well as knowledge. At one point, he stopped at the federal armory at Harper's Ferry, Virginia, to buy rifles, pistols, tomahawks, and knives to outfit his men. Later, in Philadelphia, he bought the most modern instruments available to help him plot his way across the wilderness, including compasses, **quadrants**, and **sextants**. And finally, he bought an assortment of "gifts" to trade with the Indians. Among these were handsome Indian peace medals made of silver, which displayed two clasped hands on one side and an engraving of Jefferson on the other. Lewis also bought **trinkets**—colored ribbon, glass and pewter beads, knives, and small mirrors—

that he thought the natives he met would like.

In his written instructions to Meriwether Lewis, President Jefferson went to great lengths to insist that the expedition always establish friendly relations with the Indians they met. Partly this was because the Corps of Discovery would be representing the United States. But partly it was because the president wanted them to return safely. For "in the loss of yourselves," Jefferson wrote, "we should lose also the information you will have acquired."

Lewis decided to write his old friend William Clark and ask him to join the expedition as co-commander, "in it's fatiegues, it's dangers and it's honors." Clark responded as soon he got the letter: "No man lives whith whome I would perfur to undertake Such a Trip."

Thomas Jefferson told a friend that he wanted the expedition leader to be "perfectly skilled in botany, natural history, mineralogy, astronomy, with at the same time the necessary firmness of body and mind, habits of living in the woods, and familiarity with the Indian character." Though no one exactly fit this description, Jefferson knew that Meriwether Lewis could be trained for the job.

(From their letters, and the lengthy journals both men kept on their journey, it is plain to see that they were not the world's best spellers. All the more reason to cherish the accounts they kept, for not knowing how to spell a word or compose a phrase surely made Lewis and Clark's detailed record keeping that much more difficult.)

Clark, a red-haired, 33-year-old Virginian, was the youngest of six brothers who had made names for themselves fighting the British during the Revolutionary War. Although he had been a captain in the U.S. Army, Clark had resigned his commission to work the family farm in Indiana. He was there when Lewis's letter arrived. Because he, like Lewis, was still single, Clark had no qualms about signing on with the bold mission.

At first, Lewis had promised his friend that he would be made a captain once again. That way he could receive the same salary as Lewis and be a co-commander of the expedition. However, Congress approved only a lieutenant's rank for Clark. Lewis was deeply offended by this decision, and he told his friend that as far as he was concerned, both would be captains on the trip and would receive equal pay.

The fact that the men agreed to share command, a rare arrangement in military ranks, shows how much they respected each other. (In fact, after the two returned from their adventure, Clark married and named his first son Meriwether Lewis Clark.)

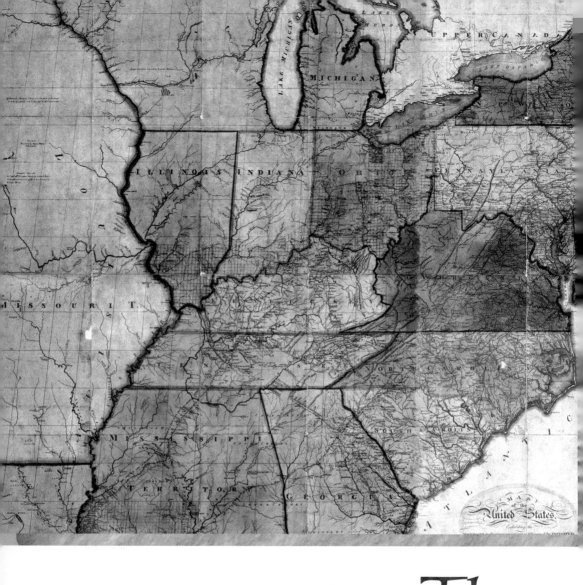

The Adventure Begins

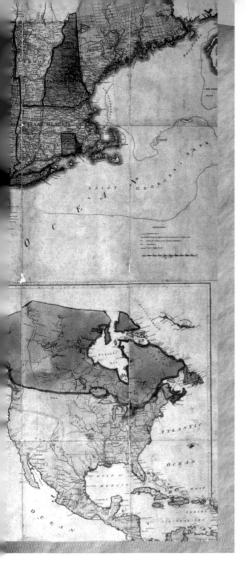

This old map shows the United States as it appeared in 1804, the year the Corps of Discovery set forth on its adventure. Lewis and Clark would explore the vast regions beyond the Mississippi River, the western boundary of U.S. settlement at that time.

3

On July 5, 1803, Lewis said farewell to Jefferson in Washington, D.C., and headed west over the mountains to Pittsburgh, Pennsylvania. There he oversaw construction of a 55-foot **keelboat** that would carry most members of the Corps of Discovery as well as their supplies. Built with an extremely shallow hull to allow it to skim over river obstacles like submerged rocks and trees, the boat could carry 10 tons of **provisions**. It had a mast for a sail and oars for rowing. It could even be towed along the riverbanks by rope if necessary.

In addition, Lewis bought another boat, called a *pirogue*, that was made by hollowing out an enormous tree trunk, perhaps 50 feet long. Their boat also had a mast and sail. And finally, it was in Pittsburgh that the Corps of Discovery's cocaptain purchased another valuable asset for the trip: a large dog of the Newfoundland breed, which he named Seaman. (The dog would later catch a live antelope crossing a stream, as well as assorted other wild game, which made him a truly welcome addition. Lewis was so fond of Seaman that, when the dog was stolen in the wilderness, he tracked the Indians who were responsible for two miles to get the animal back.)

Lewis left Pittsburgh in October and boated down the Ohio River to meet up with William Clark. Clark had also been recruiting men for the expedition.

> **While he traveled from Pittsburgh to St. Louis, Meriwether Lewis continued searching for "good hunters, stout, healthy, unmarried men, accustomed to the woods, and capable of bearing bodily fatigue in a pretty considerable degree."**

Joining them was Clark's black slave, who was named York. He would prove to be of great interest to the Indians along the trek. Many were fascinated by York's dark skin. Together, Lewis and Clark headed to St. Louis and the mouth of the Missouri River.

Most of the men who joined the Corps of Discovery were civilians. But because the expedition was being paid for by the U.S. government, they were required to enlist as soldiers.

It was now December 1803, and although the Corps of Discovery's voyage had technically begun, Lewis and Clark knew that they couldn't continue up the Missouri until springtime. They used the winter months to continue enlisting men for the mission.

Clark set up a base camp, which came to be known as Camp Dubois (or Camp Wood), opposite the mouth of the Missouri River in present-day Illinois. After building a small fort fitted with several cabins, he began training his men. He taught them the skills they would need on the trip. Lewis and Clark also began recording notes in their diaries about river conditions, reports from other river travelers about the Missouri's geography, and information from local Indians.

Approximately 40 soldiers and several French guides formed the initial Corps of Discovery at Camp Dubois. The captains never intended for everyone to travel with them all the way to the Pacific coast. Some were expected to go as far as possible with the keelboat, then return with it to St. Louis, carrying reports of the group's initial progress and samples of plants and animals. By April of 1804, the permanent crew numbered 33. Little is known about most of them, except that they came from various states: Kentucky, Indiana, Virginia, Connecticut, Maryland, Massachusetts, New Hampshire, North Carolina, Pennsylvania, and Vermont.

If the Corps of Discovery succeeded, its members looked forward to gratitude from the U.S. government. In a letter dated April 8, 1804, Corps of Discovery member John Ordway wrote to his parents: "I am now on an expidition to the westward, with Capt. Lewis and Capt. Clark. . . . We are to ascend the Missouri River with a boat as far as it is navigable and then to go by land, to the western ocean, if nothing prevents . . . and if we make Great Discoveries as we expect, the United States has promised to make us Great Rewards."

Finally, on May 14, 1804, Lewis and Clark were

ready for the real beginning of their quest for the Northwest Passage. In the morning, Clark wrote that they were "fixing for a Start." By afternoon that same day, he and his crew were heading up the mouth of the Missouri River. "I set out at 4 oClock P.M. in the presence of many of the Neighbouring inhabitents, and proceeded on under a jentle brease up the Missouri," he wrote.

At this point, Clark had high hopes of reaching the Pacific Ocean by June or July at the latest, and arriving back in St. Louis by November or December of 1804. Based on information and existing maps he had gathered, he had come up with amazingly accurate estimates of how long the journey up the known stretches of the Missouri would take. But as for the vast wilderness that lay beyond, including the imposing Rocky Mountains, Clark really had no inkling how much farther the journey would be, or how long and treacherous a trail the Corps of Discovery would have to blaze.

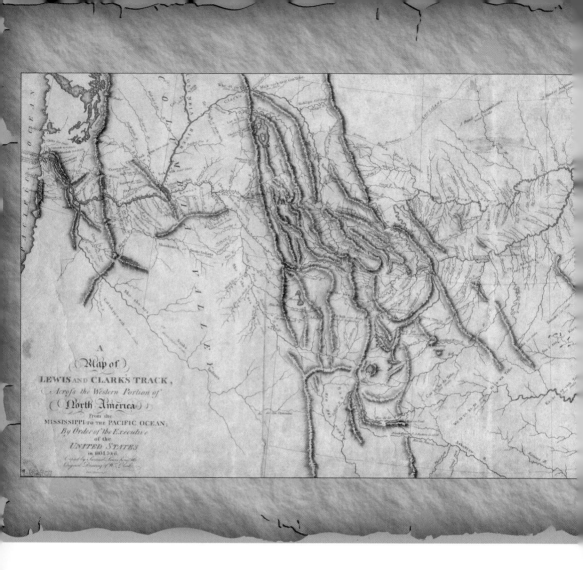

Exploring the Missouri River

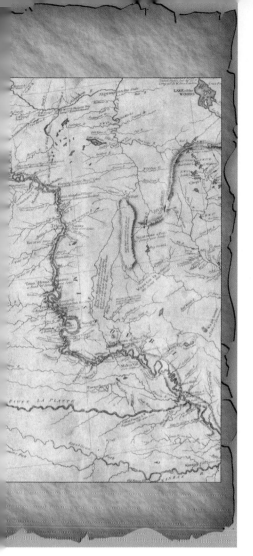

During their expedition, Lewis and Clark took careful notes about the places they visited and the people they met. They also carefully charted their route west. After Lewis and Clark returned, their notes were used to create very detailed and accurate maps, such as the one from 1814 shown here.

4

he Mississippi River might be mightier, but the Missouri (often called "the Big Muddy") had its own fickle currents. The Corps of Discovery was traveling upriver, against the current. The exploring party's three boats were propelled not by motors, but by manpower (and occasionally, wind). This meant that for much of their trip northwestward, they could not relax their efforts for a moment or their boats would begin drifting back downstream. That was bad enough for the two pirogues, but it made maneuvering the huge keel boat especially troublesome.

The men had three ways of propelling their crafts upriver: rowing the awkward boats with oars; moving them forward with long, wooden poles that they would push off the river bottom; or towing the heavy wooden hulks with ropes pulled by men onshore. If you've ever tried any of these ways to move a boat, you can imagine how backbreaking the work was. Remember, too, that it was summertime, and terribly hot. Worse, as Lewis and Clark would write in their journals, there were ravenous insects, particularly mosquitoes, that constantly swarmed around the hapless crew members. "Ticks and Musquiters are verry troublesome," Clark noted.

Still, by July 21, the expedition had traveled 642 miles up the Missouri, averaging about 10 miles a day. Several days later, the captains stopped their journey long enough to climb a steep bluff and gaze out over the "most butifull prospect of the River up & Down . . . which I ever beheld." They were viewing the seemingly endless prairies of the upper Midwest, foot-tall grasslands that stretched as "fur as Can be seen."

Thirty years after Lewis and Clark's expedition, an artist named George Catlin painted many of the scenes the explorers had discovered. This Catlin painting shows the spot along the Missouri River where Lewis and Clark buried Sergeant Charles Floyd, who died during the expedition.

Late in August, the crew members had to deal with the one and only fatality of their party the entire trip. Sergeant Charles Floyd became severely ill and, despite the best "treatments" available to his wilderness physicians—bleedings and Benjamin

Rush's laxatives—he died. People have speculated that his death was caused by a burst appendix, which no doctor in the world could have successfully treated at the time. He was buried atop a *bluff* near a river his comrades named in his honor.

Lewis and Clark began writing about sightings of new and strange animals, including prairie dogs,

The Teton Sioux were fierce warriors and hunters. Like other Plains Indians, they depended on the large buffalo herds to provide food, and used the furry hides of the animals to make clothes and shelter.

coyotes, pronghorn antelopes, jackrabbits, mule deer, and badgers. Other creatures, such as buffalo, astonished the travelers because of their huge numbers—as many as 10,000 in a single herd. And although Lewis and Clark were now in the High Plains, which were not quite as fertile as the lower elevations, the captains continued to describe the countryside as "Well-watered and beautiful."

Before long, the Corps of Discovery encountered an Indian tribe that was feared even by other Indians throughout the region—the Teton Sioux. The Sioux were famous for charging fellow Indians and European fur trappers and traders high "tolls" to pass through their territory. After meeting Lewis and Clark and receiving assorted gifts from them, the Sioux demanded one of the Corps' pirogues and all its contents in exchange for letting the party continue. The captains refused, and only by drawing their weapons and bracing for an attack did they convince the Indians to back off. Lewis later referred to them as "the vilest miscreants of the savage race" and the "pirates of the Missouri."

By October 25, the explorers had reached their winter destination and the last known settlement on existing maps: the Mandan Indian village. They had

George Catlin made this painting of the Mandan village
where the Corps of Discovery spent the winter of 1804.

spent 164 days and come an estimated 1,600 miles
to reach this point. It turned out to be a perfect site
to make a winter camp. The Mandans were a peace-
ful, primarily agricultural tribe that lived in earthen
lodges along the Missouri River. But because of the
periodic raids of neighboring Sioux warriors and a
devastating smallpox epidemic that had broken out
several years earlier, the Mandans had lost a great

many members of their tribe. In his journals, Clark called them "the most friendly, well disposed Indians inhabiting the Missouri. They are brave, humane, and hospitable."

The expedition members built their winter fort opposite the Mandan village in what is now North Dakota. The sturdy structure would be all that separated the men from fierce winter winds and temperatures that dropped to 40 degrees below zero. Throughout the five long months they spent there, the men hunted for food (the group could eat a buffalo, several deer, and an elk in a single day), repaired their worn equipment, and socialized with the Mandan.

It was also among the Mandan that Lewis and Clark discovered their expedition's most valuable member: Sacagawea. She was the wife of a French-Canadian trader named Toussaint Charbonneau, who was living with the Mandan. Lewis invited them to join the Corps of Discovery because of their knowledge of other Indian tribes farther upriver. Sacagawea was a Shoshone Indian by birth, but at age 13 she had been captured by warriors from the Hidatsa tribe. In February of 1805, while the Corps was wintering at Fort Mandan, Sacagawea gave birth to a boy she named Jean Baptiste. Incredibly, she then carried the infant all the way to the Pacific coast and back. Her addition to the trip was very important, largely because her presence indicated to Indian tribes along the way that they had nothing to fear from the American explorers. War parties never included women.

As winter drew to a close, the members of the Corps of Discovery made plans to continue their trek into unknown territory. Beforehand, though, the party split up. About one-quarter of the original crew was sent back to St. Louis in the keelboat. Their important job was to ensure that the notes Lewis and Clark had written so far made their way back to President Jefferson, who was anxiously awaiting word of his expedition.

Also sent back were assorted examples of plant life that Lewis had collected on the journey so far: Indian tobacco, sagebrush, and cottonwood. In addition, animal skins were packed, and live animals were boxed up for the president. These included four magpies and the lone prairie dog that crew members had managed to flush out of its burrow. Finally, written descriptions and artifacts from various Indian tribes were boxed up for the president's inspection, as were maps.

In some respects, the first leg of the journey that had brought them this far—despite being potentially dangerous—was the easy part. Other white men had made the journey before them, mapping the way and meeting with the Indians along the river. The Corps of Discovery had not yet broken new ground. But from this point forward, they were truly heading into the unknown, with only the vaguest notions of what awaited them.

Nevertheless, the captains were eager to continue their quest. It was now nearly a full year since they had left their first fort at Camp Dubois. Already they were far behind Clark's timetable to complete the trip. One passage written by Meriwether Lewis on April 7, 1805, sums up his excitement about again getting under way:

> We were now about to penetrate a country at least two thousand miles in width, on which the foot of civillized man had never trodden. . . . Entertain[in]g as I do, the most confident hope of succeading in a voyage which had formed a da[r]ling project of mine for the last ten years, I could but esteem this moment of my departure as among the most happy of my life.

Into the Wilderness

Sacagawea, the Shoshone Indian whom Lewis and Clark met among the Mandan villagers, was one of the most valuable members of the Corps of Discovery. She helped to guide the Americans through the Northwest.

5

It was a clear, cold morning on April 7 when the St. Louis–bound crew members headed down the Missouri. But by the time the permanent party was ready to continue westward, it was 4 P.M. and a comfortable 64 degrees. In all, 33 persons were continuing up the Missouri in search of its **headwaters**: Lewis and Clark, three sergeants, two French-Canadian interpreters, 23 privates, the slave York, and Sacagawea and her infant son.

The party moved westward into what is now Montana. They noticed that the landscape was changing from the lush, grassy plains farther south to more rugged country typical of high-plains deserts. The animal sightings changed as well. For the first time, the group saw bighorn sheep, majestic creatures with curling horns. But even more impressive was their first glimpse of America's largest *predator*–the grizzly bear.

In late May, after several weeks of struggling against the Missouri's increasingly swifter and shallower currents, the leaders of the Corps of Discovery went ashore to scout the terrain. While standing atop a hill, Lewis saw rising mountain peaks in the distance. He thought these must surely be the Rocky Mountains. Little did he know, he was observing the Bears Paw Mountains. The mighty Rockies were still 100 miles farther west.

But he and Clark realized that they were close to accomplishing the first phase of their mission: finding the headwaters of the Missouri River. What they didn't realize was that to do so, they would have to solve a puzzle farther upstream.

In early June they found another river, now called the Marias, merging with the Missouri. The

*D*espite warnings, the Corps of Discovery members were actually eager to encounter grizzly bears. In late April, they got their first chance. Two grizzlies were spotted near the Yellowstone River. After the men wounded both of them, one enraged bear began chasing Lewis, who barely

managed to reload his gun in time and kill the beast. "The Indians may well fear this animal . . . but in the hands of a skillful rifleman they are by no means as formidable or dangerous as they have been represented," he wrote confidently after his first brush with grizzlies. But he would soon change his opinion of the West's most feared predator. A week later, he and several men emptied their guns on one tough bear, with little initial effect. And after another bear shooting, Lewis wrote, "I must confess that I do not like the gentlemen and had rather fight two Indians than one bear."

question they faced was, which branch should they follow? The Indians they had met had not told them about the branches. If they guessed wrong, they could lose valuable time heading up the wrong waterway. That might mean being trapped in the forebidding Rockies for another winter.

After scouting ahead along the left branch, Lewis and several men were relieved to discover the Great Falls of the Missouri, a breathtaking landmark the Indians had told him he would come across. He called the falls the "grandest sight I ever beheld."

Beautiful though they were, the falls presented a major obstacle: the Corps of Discovery would have to find a way to *portage* (carry boats) around them. Clark estimated that going around the falls, with all the expedition's boats and equipment, would require a portage of 18 miles. They decided to leave the two pirogues behind, and the equipment that was not absolutely necessary was buried near the falls for retrieval on the way home.

The men made wagon frames out of the boats' masts and nearby cottonwood trees and used the wagons to transport the vessels, which now consisted of several Indian-made canoes. But since they had no horses, the men pulled the wagons by hand—

incredibly difficult and backbreaking labor. Worse, the ground was covered with prickly pear cactus, the spines of which easily pierced the men's elk-skin moccasins and clothing.

In addition, the weather was changing on a moment's notice. Scorching heat would be interrupted by violent wind and hailstorms, some so fierce they actually pelted the men bloody. Although the men were tired, "no one complains, all go with cheerfullness," wrote Lewis.

Before the men knew it, a month had gone by as they completed the portage. Although he didn't confide in anyone but his own journal, Lewis was beginning to have grave doubts about whether the party would make it through the Rockies, then to the Pacific Ocean, and back again to the Mandan village before winter.

Beyond the falls, the Corps of Discovery found a magnificent canyon they called the Gates of the Mountains, which was at the foot of the Rockies. Sacagawea, who had been captured as a teenager in this exact area years earlier, began to notice familiar landmarks, particularly the three forks (branches) that fed the headwaters of the Missouri.

Lewis and Clark decided to name the rivers the

"I beheld the Rocky Mountains for the first time." wrote Lewis. "But when I reflected on the difficulties which this snowey barrier would most probably throw in my way to the Pacific . . . it in some measure counter-balanced the joy I had felt in the first few minutes I gazed at them."

Jefferson, the Madison, and the Gallatin (the latter two after the president's secretary of state, James Madison, and treasury secretary Albert Gallatin).

On July 30, some of the men went up the Jefferson branch. They had been told that eventually they could make a "short" portage over the Continental Divide (which separates the river systems east and west of the Rockies). Meanwhile, Lewis went overland to find Shoshone Indians from whom he could buy horses. He and his men came to what they decided was the source of the Missouri River, at this point little more than a stream. Soon the captain's worst fears came true. From high on a nearby ridge, he saw not the grassy plains leading west to the Columbia River—which is what he hoped to see—but mountain ranges extending to the horizon.

Lewis did finally meet with the Shoshone. He convinced them to return with him to the camp where Clark and the others were waiting. There, much to everyone's surprise, Sacagawea recognized the Shoshone chief Cameahwait as her long-lost brother. Their reunion made it much easier for Lewis and Clark to buy the horses they needed to continue westward. Another reason the Shoshone were eager to help was because Lewis and Clark promised them that the United States would later supply guns with which they could fight their enemies, the Sioux and the Blackfeet.

The Final Push

"Explorers at the Portage," a sculpture of Lewis and Clark, overlooks the Missouri and Sun Rivers near Great Falls, Montana. Today, Meriwether Lewis and William Clark are remembered as brave American heroes. Their expedition was so well planned and executed that, despite numerous hardships, only one member of the Corps of Discovery was lost.

6

The going would get tougher before it got easier for the Corps of Discovery. Ahead of them stood the Bitterroot Range, a stretch of the Rockies that separates what are now the states of Montana and Idaho. The nearby Salmon River flowed toward the Columbia River, which Lewis and Clark desperately wanted to reach. But a scouting trip proved that the Salmon was too swift and rough to float downstream. Making matters worse, sheer cliffs along its banks ruled out any notions of following the river's course on land. No wonder people would later refer to the Salmon River as "the River of No Return."

As if things weren't bad enough, food was becoming scarce in the rugged terrain. Realizing the hopelessness of this route, Lewis and Clark decided to attempt to cross the mountains on horseback under the guidance of a Shoshone named Old Toby.

On August 30, 1805, they set out on one of the worst stretches of the entire expedition. Although they now had 30 horses, most were used to carry the equipment the explorers still needed. One crew member described the passage as "Horrid bad going," and for good reason. Although a passing Indian had told them they were no more than five days' march from a river that did lead to the Columbia, the tortuous stretch down the west side of the Bitterroot took twice that long.

As often happens in the western high country, winter was already setting in, though it was only mid-September. The deepening snows made passage along the narrow, rocky trails a nerve-racking ordeal. Several horses slid down the steep mountain sides to their deaths, taking valuable equipment with them. In addition, food was now so scarce that the men had to resort to eating several of the packhorses. And Old Toby wasn't always the expert guide the group had hoped. More than once he missed the correct trails and forced the expedition to backtrack until they found their way. Clark, normally not one to complain about adversity, now wrote in his journal, "I have been wet and as cold in every part as I ever was in my life." He feared that his feet would freeze in the thin elk-skin moccasins. "To describe the road of this day," he said, "would be a repitition of yesterday excpt the Snow which made it much wors[e]."

Not long after the men slaughtered their last expendable packhorse, Clark returned from a short scouting mission with dried salmon and roots he had been given from Indians down on the prairie. Lewis and Clark didn't know whether to celebrate or be disappointed about their situation. On the one hand, they knew that the worst of the mountain passage was behind. On the other hand, they also knew there was no easy Northwest Passage to the Pacific.

They forged ahead, traveling by canoe along the rivers that led to the Columbia. The land was desertlike, with sparse vegetation and little to eat.

When the Corps grew weary of eating dried salmon and plant roots—the diet of local Native Americans—they began buying dogs from the Indians as food.

On October 16, the welcome Columbia was finally in sight. A week later, though, the explorers had to run the most treacherous stretches of river on the entire trek. Much to the local Indians' surprise, Lewis and Clark and their men survived the swirling rapids unscathed. Soon they left the desert behind and entered the lush, nearly tropical evergreen forests of the Pacific Northwest (where average rainfall is nearly five times the amount on the plains).

As the party moved on, the men saw obvious signs that other white men had come before them from the west coast: the Native Americans there wore clothing acquired from sailors, and they were fond of using English swear words.

At long last, on November 7, 1805, the Corps of Discovery paddled into a huge bay where the Columbia entered the Pacific Ocean. "Ocean in view! O! the joy!" wrote Lewis.

After traveling an estimated 4,118 miles (by Clark's surprisingly accurate reckoning), the expedition built a winter fort on the south side of the bay. Unlike the Mandan village fort, though, the crew

Lewis and Clark respected many of the Native Americans they met. Fifteen years after the expedition, a group of chiefs from a midwestern tribe visited St. Louis. The one in the front of this painting is wearing one of the peace medals distributed by Lewis and Clark.

members did not like their new winter home at Fort Clatsop. Two things annoyed them: the constantly rainy weather and the local Indians. Years of trading with ships in search of furs and other goods had made these Indians shrewd bargainers. Lewis and Clark all but called them thieves. And Sergeant

Gass wrote, "All the Indians from the Rocky Mountains to the falls of Columbia, are an honest, ingenious and well disposed people; but from the falls to the seacoast, and along it, they are a rascally, thieving set."

What did the men do all winter? They repaired equipment, boiled seawater to get salt, hunted for food, and made an amazing 338 pairs of elk-skin moccasins for the return trip. Meanwhile, Clark spent much of his time drawing detailed maps of the journey westward from Fort Mandan. If a ship had sailed into the bay that winter, the men were prepared to seek passage on it to return home by sea. Unfortunately for them, no ships from any country came to the mouth of the Columbia that winter.

By late March, the entire party had had enough of the Pacific coast, and they eagerly set out on the return trip. The late arrival of spring in the Rockies slowed their journey considerably. But by July they were near the Continental Divide, and for the first time, the group split up so that Clark could explore the Yellowstone River while Lewis sought a shortcut to the winding route of the upper Missouri River. With a hint of concern for each other's safety, the men parted after agreeing to meet where the Yellowstone enters the Missouri.

Thanks to Lewis's excursion, an overland route was discovered that was 600 miles and well over a month shorter than the route they had taken westward. But Lewis also had his closest brush with death on this part of journey. One morning, after camping out with Blackfeet Indians, Lewis and several of his men awoke to the sight of the Blackfeet trying to steal their guns and horses. In the struggle that followed, one Indian was stabbed to death, and Lewis fatally shot another, who managed to fire back. The shot barely missed the captain's head.

In mid-August, the Corps of Discovery reached the Mandan village, and Lewis celebrated his 32nd birthday. But back east, many Americans had given the expedition up for lost. Thus it came as quite a surprise when the weary trav-

Although the Indians didn't shoot Meriwether Lewis, the captain wasn't lucky enough to dodge a bullet fired by one of his own men. He was heading south to meet up with Clark's party when he was shot in the buttocks by a Corps member who had mistaken him for an elk. Fortunately, the wound was not life-threatening— just embarrassing.

The cocaptains of the successful expedition had very different fates. Meriwether Lewis killed himself in 1809, just three years after the Corps of Discovery returned. His partner William Clark (opposite) held important government posts and lived into his late 60s.

elers finally rode their boats down into St. Louis. They were greeted by cheering crowds.

Lewis and Clark were cheered throughout America when news of their return spread eastward.

And they rightfully basked in the glow of their accomplishment. Clark would go on to be appointed superintendent of Indian Affairs for the United States, get married, and raise a family. Lewis, who served briefly as governor of the Louisiana Territory, did not spend his remaining days as productively. He never even began to publish his journals of the trip. (Neither did Clark, for that matter, until he gave them to a writer to publish in 1814.)

For reasons unknown, Lewis began to grow depressed in the years after his epic adventure. He began drinking heavily. Only three years after the end of his great expedition, while traveling through Tennessee on his way to Washington, he shot himself to death. His precious journals weren't published until the 20th century, when Americans of all ages thrilled at the descriptions of how their nation's greatest explorers found the gateway to the West.

Chronology

1770 William Clark born August 1 in Caroline County, Virginia.

1774 Meriwether Lewis born August 18 in Locust Hill, Virginia.

1803 President Thomas Jefferson enlists Lewis and Clark to go on an expedition up the Missouri River in search of the Northwest Passage to the Pacific Ocean. In December, Lewis and Clark build Camp Dubois near St. Louis.

1804 In April, the Corps of Discovery begins the journey up the Missouri River. By November, Lewis and Clark build Fort Mandan near an Indian village.

1805 In April, three-quarters of the corps members proceed westward up the Missouri while the remaining men head back down the river with diaries, maps, and plant and animal specimens for Jefferson. In June, the men make an 18-mile portage around the Great Falls of the Missouri. In September and October, the expedition manages to cross the Continental Divide as winter sets in and also navigates treacherous rapids along the Columbia River. In November, the Corps of Discovery reaches the Pacific Ocean, where Fort Clatsop is built as a winter camp.

1806 In late March, the expedition begins heading back to St. Louis. On the return trip, Lewis is nearly killed by an Indian in a skirmish and shot in the rump by one of his own men in a hunting accident. In September, Lewis and Clark return triumphantly to St. Louis.

1809 Meriwether Lewis dies.

1838 William Clark dies.

Glossary

astronomy—the study of stars and planets.

bluff—a high, steep bank or cliff.

botany—the study of plants.

commission—to appoint or assign to a task.

corps—a group of people, often in the military, who share a mission or common goal.

expedition—a journey that is made for a specific purpose, such as exploration.

headwaters—the source of a stream or river.

keelboat—a riverboat with a very shallow hull that can be rowed, pulled, towed, or sailed.

laxative—a food or drug that is taken to cause a bowel movement.

pirogue—a dugout boat resembling a large canoe.

portage—to carry boats or supplies overland from one body of water to another

predator—an animal that kills other animals for food.

provisions—a stock of supplies, especially food.

quadrant—an instrument shaped like one-quarter of a circle, used for measuring the position of stars.

secretary—a person employed to handle correspondence and other routine business for another person.

sextant—an instrument used to establish location by measuring how high above the horizon certain stars are.

trek—a difficult journey.

trinkets—small ornaments or items of little value that explorers carried to trade with natives they encountered.

Further Reading

Ambrose, Stephen E. *Undaunted Courage: Meriwether Lewis, Thomas Jefferson, and the Opening of the American West.* New York: Simon & Schuster, 1996.

Cavan, Seamus. *Lewis and Clark and the Route to the Pacific.* New York: Chelsea House Publishers, 1991.

Duncan, Dayton, and Burns, Ken. *Lewis and Clark: The Journey of the Corps of Discovery.* New York: Alfred A. Knopf, 1997.

Holloway, David. *Lewis and Clark, and the Crossing of North America.* New York: Saturday Review Press, 1974.

Picture Credits

RICHARD KOZAR has written several Chelsea House books, including biographies of Hillary Rodham Clinton and Elizabeth Dole. He is also the author of *Daniel Boone and the Exploration of the Frontier* in the EXPLORERS OF NEW WORLDS series. He lives in Whitney, Pennsylvania, with his wife, Heidi, and daughters Caty and Macy.

DATE DUE

MAR 1 9					
NOV 8					
MAR 2 3					

HIGHSMITH #45228